MUD TURTLI
GUIDE

TURTLE AS PETS

Complete Owners Guide On Raising And Caring
Of Turtle For Beginners: Training, Feeding,
Health, Reproduction, Housing And much More

Marilyn Lori

Table of Contents

CHAPTER ONE

Mud Turtle

Introduction

Mud turtles are tiny turtles belonging to the Kinosternidae family. North America, Central America, and South America are home to this species. Mud turtles inhabit wetlands, waterways, ponds, and marshes. They inhabit a diversity of habitats but prefer shallow, sluggish water and sediment. The average length of these tortoises is 5-7 inches, and they can live up to 25 years in the open. Most mud turtles have dark shells and are frequently confused with other species of turtles.

Mud turtles are omnivores, meaning they consume both flora and animals. They consume insects, larvae, worms, crustaceans, amphibians, and fish. In addition to aquatic vegetation, they consume fruits and seeds.

Mud turtles are reclusive and do not interact with other turtles frequently. During their reproductive season, females deposit eggs in colonies on the shore. The ova typically emerge in approximately two months, and the juvenile turtles reach maturity at approximately one year of age.

The mud turtle is not considered to be in danger of extinction. However, owing to habitat degradation, pollution, and hunting, their populations are declining. To protect these animals and their habitats, conservation efforts are made.

Description

Mud turtles are North American freshwater turtles that are diminutive in size. They inhabit shallow, slow-moving bodies of water, such as marshes and wetlands. They favor areas with a marshy, porous substrate and abundant vegetation.

The carapace of a mud turtle is typically ovoid and dark brown or black. Markings on the shell may be yellow, orange, or white. Additionally, the cranium, neck, and legs have yellow, orange, or white patterns and patches. The carapace or outermost exoskeleton can have three distinct ridges.

The mud turtle's flippers are webbed and its neck is extended. It possesses small pupils and a brief muzzle. It is a timid species that is seldom observed out of the water.

Omnivorous, mud turtles consume insects, crustaceans, fish, and plant matter. They are also known to consume carcasses.

Mud turtles are abundant in the environment and can be found in the majority of North

American regions. Due to their propensity to graze on aquatic vegetation, they may be considered a nuisance in certain areas.

Popular as pets, mud turtles can be kept in captivity so long as their natural habitat is maintained. A large aquarium with a layer of porous, muddy substrate and a few inches of water is required.

Additionally, a basking area should be provided. They require little maintenance and can live up to 25 years in captivity.

History And Origin

It is believed that the mud turtle originated in the southeastern United States, where it is most abundant. Since then, the species has spread throughout the United States, Mexico, and Central America.

It is believed that human activity introduced it to some regions, such as Hawaii.

Mud turtles have existed for millions of years, and their fossils have been discovered in Eocene-era deposits. The mud turtle is the only known member of the Kinosternon genus, which is believed to have diverged from other turtle genera around 35 million years ago.

Mud turtles are diminutive turtles, averaging between five and seven inches in length. They have smooth, ovoid shells that range from brown to olive green in color. The upper shell is characterized by three distinct ridges, while the lower shell is typically flat. The mud turtle's epidermis is also dark and may contain microscopic yellow patches.

Mud turtles are omnivorous, consuming both plant and animal matter. They have been observed consuming snails, invertebrates, nematodes, tadpoles, and other aquatic organisms. Additionally, they consume flora such as algae, aquatic plants, and fruits.

Males and females of mud turtles only interact during mating season. Males are typically larger than females and can be distinguished by their longer, more robust tails. Typically, the mating season occurs during the spring and summer. Females deposit two to four eggs in a nest, which they will secure until they hatch. Typically, the embryos require two to three months to emerge.

According to the IUCN Red List of Threatened Species, mud turtles are classified as Least Concern. Even though they are not endangered by extinction, habitat loss and the pet trade pose a threat to them. In most jurisdictions, it is illegal to capture native mud turtles.

CHAPTER TWO

Physical Characteristics

Mud turtles are small aquatic turtles that inhabit North, Central, and South American freshwater habitats. In addition to their dark, olive-brown, or black carapace, they have a yellow or orange plastron that is divided into two sections. On average, mud turtles are 5 to 10 centimeters long and weigh up to 200 grams. The structure of the carapace of mud turtles varies greatly between species. Some mud turtles have shells that are smooth and flat, while others have dome-shaped shells.

Mud turtles have short, robust necks and lengthy, robust fins. In addition to stripes or patches of yellow, orange, or red on the head and neck, mud turtles have a pair of barbels on either side of the neck.

Mud turtles have webbed and clawed feet that enable them to ascend and burrow.

The color patterns of mud turtles vary widely, ranging from dark brown to olive green. The plastron of the mud turtle is divided into two sections and is yellow or orange in color. The plastron may have yellow or orange margins, as well as patches or stripes of other hues. The scutes of the carapace can also have other colored patches or patterns.

Mud turtles are omnivores and consume a wide range of nutrients, including worms, invertebrates, crustaceans, fish, and plant matter. They are also known to consume carcasses. They are primarily nocturnal and spend the majority of their time in the water. During the winter, mud turtles are capable of hibernating, and they often conceal themselves in the dirt or sediment at the bottom of a lagoon or lake.

Shell And Head

The mud turtle's carapace is typically dark brown or black, with yellow or orange stripes running the length of its body. Its cranium is typically dark, but depending on the species, it may be paler. The mud turtle has a long neck and a distinctive spade-shaped pattern on its carapace. The mud turtle's carapace is covered in a dense layer of sludge and vegetation, allowing it to blend in with its surroundings.

Dietary staples for the mud turtle include flora, small invertebrates, and carrion. The mud turtle is an active predator that utilizes its extended neck to capture prey. It is an opportunistic omnivore, consuming whatever it can locate.

Mud turtles are typically reclusive creatures that avoid other turtles. Typically, they are not combative and will retreat when confronted.

However, when confronted or hounded, they can become aggressive.

Typically, mud turtles inhabit shallow, murky water. They favor slow-moving water and typically bask on boulders and driftwood in the sun. During the hot summer months, they frequently conceal themselves in the dirt to keep cool.

Although mud turtles are not considered endangered, habitat destruction and water pollution pose a threat to their survival. They are also susceptible to predators such as raccoons, skunks, and raptors.

The mud turtle is an integral part of its ecosystem, as its diet of microscopic invertebrates and carrion helps to keep the water pure. It is also a significant source of nutrition for fish and fowl, among other species.

Limbs And Tail

Mud turtles are a species of turtle distributed throughout the southeastern United States in freshwater habitats. They are diminutive, with an average carapace length of 7 inches. Carapaces of mud turtles are robust, dome-shaped, and dark brown to black in color. The carapace has yellow, orange, or red stripes and patches.

The mud turtle has four legs. For swimming, the forelimbs are paddle-shaped with webbed or scalloped toes. The turtle's hind extremities are marginally larger and have a longer, more powerful claw that aids in movement on land.

The tails of mud turtles are between one-third and one-half the length of their carapace. The tip of the tail is slender and tapered.

It is utilized for strolling balance and swimming propulsion.

Mud turtles spend the majority of their time in the water but are capable of basking on land. They consume aquatic vegetation and animals such as insects, nematodes, mollusks, and crustaceans. They have also been observed feeding on deceased turtles and other carrion.

In certain regions, mud turtles are considered endangered due to habitat degradation, pollution, and predation by larger animals. In some jurisdictions, collecting or possessing mud turtles is prohibited. To ensure their survival, it is essential to protect these tortoises and their habitats.

Coloration

Mud turtles are diminutive reptiles measuring between 4 and 7 inches in length. They have a carapace that is either olive green or brown and is compressed. The carapace (the upper portion of the exoskeleton) is typically marked with yellow, orange, or brown patches and lines. The plastron (the underside of the shell) is yellow or cream-colored, and some specimens have dark spots in the center. Their head, neck, and extremities are brown with stripes and patches of yellow or orange. The eye color is yellow.

Typically, mud turtles inhabit freshwater habitats such as slow-moving streams and shallow pools. Additionally, they inhabit marshes, wetlands, and ponds. They favor murky, shallow waters rich in vegetation and small animals like frogs, tadpoles, and crustaceans.

Due to their coloring, mud turtles are well-camouflaged in their natural habitat. The carapace is typically olive green or brown with yellow, orange, or reddish-brown patches and lines.

This assists the mud turtle in blending in with its surroundings. The plastron is yellow or cream-colored, with dark smudges in the center of some specimens. Additionally camouflaged, the head, neck, and extremities are brown with yellow or orange stripes and patches. The eye color is yellow. This coloring helps the mud turtle merge in with its surroundings and prevents it from being readily spotted by potential predators.

The mud turtle is a unique species that has adapted well to its environment. Their coloring helps them conceal themselves from potential predators and affords them some protection. They can also persist in a variety of habitats, including marshes, wetlands, and slow-moving streams. Mud turtles are a distinct species that can be readily identified in the environment due to their distinct coloring.

CHAPTER THREE

Lifespan

Small aquatic tortoises are found in North and Central America. They are semi-aquatic, which means that they spend some time in the water and some time on land. They are omnivores and consume both animals and vegetation.

In captivity, mud turtles can live to be over 20 years old, but in the open, their average longevity is much shorter due to predation and other environmental factors. They can live anywhere from 10 to 15 years in the open, but the majority do not survive past the age of five.

Mud turtles attain sexual maturity between the ages of five and seven years. Generally, mating occurs in the spring, and nesting occurs in the summer.

Females deposit their eggs in the water or near the water's margin in damp sediment. Typically, embryos emerge in about two months.

Mud turtles are endangered due to habitat loss and overexploitation for the pet trade. In addition, they are simple prey for predators, who frequently harvest their eggs for sustenance.

In general, mud turtles have a comparatively lengthy lifespan, with some individuals surviving in captive for over 20 years. In the wild, however, they are more susceptible to predation and other environmental factors and have shortened lifespans.

Habitat And Care

Mud Turtles are aquatic turtles indigenous to North and Central America. Typically, their length ranges between 4 and 7 inches.

They are readily identified by their brown, black, or olive shells, as well as their vibrant yellow and orange markings.

Mud Turtles are semi-aquatic, which means they spend the majority of their time in the water but can also be found on land. They inhabit habitats ranging from modest marshes to deep wetlands and ponds. They favor murky, sluggish waters and are frequently located in and around submerged debris and vegetation. Also known to inhabit slow-moving streams and rivers are Mud Turtles.

Mud Turtles are omnivorous in the environment, meaning they consume both flora and animals. Their diet consists of aquatic vegetation, such as algae and duckweed, and tiny invertebrates, such as insects, worms, snails, and crustaceans.

Typically, Mud Turtles are reclusive and do not interact with one another. Nevertheless, they may congregate during mating season, which typically occurs in the spring and summer.

In captivity, Mud Turtles need an environment that closely resembles their natural habitat. They should be furnished with an aquarium containing at least 50 liters of water and a basking area. To provide concealing places and visual stimulation, the aquarium should be adorned with pebbles, debris, and other natural embellishments. The water should be filtered and maintained at a temperature between 70 and 75 degrees Fahrenheit.

Additionally, Mud Turtles should be fed a variety of nutrients, including insects, fish, nematodes, and aquatic vegetation. They should be fed every other day, with calcium and vitamin supplements supplementing their diet.

Mud Turtles are simple to maintain and make excellent companions. Some may live for up to 25 years. Before taking on the responsibility of providing for a Mud Turtle, prospective proprietors should therefore conduct extensive research.

Natural Habitat

The Mud Turtle is a species of aquatic turtle found in North and Central American freshwater habitats. Typically, these turtles inhabit sluggish, slow-moving rivers and streams, as well as modest ponds, marshes, and lakes. Mud Turtles seek shelter and sustenance in areas with abundant aquatic vegetation, such as lily pads. Additionally, they inhabit brackish water, such as estuaries and coastal regions.

Mud Turtles are typically located in shallow water, but they are capable of diving to greater depths when necessary. They are frequently observed basking on boulders and logs near the water's edge. Even when basking in the sun, they are less likely to do so than other tortoises.

From the southeastern United States to Central America and as far south as Peru, the range of the Mud Turtle is extensive. They are abundant in the southeastern United States, but habitat degradation is reducing their range.

Mud Turtles are omnivores and will consume invertebrates, aquatic vegetation, crustaceans, mollusks, and small fish. They also consume carrion and occasionally scavenge at the water's bottom.

Mud Turtles are typically reclusive creatures, but they will occasionally bask in groups. Males are territorial and may engage other males in combat. Also, territorial, females will establish a territory around the nesting site.

Females will also safeguard their embryos aggressively from predators.

Some individuals of the Mud Turtle have been observed to live up to 50 years in the open. In late spring and early summer, females deposit up to three clusters of eggs annually. Usually deposited in saturated soil or sand, it takes between 60 and 90 days for the embryos to emerge. Juvenile turtles are diminutive and readily confused with adult mud turtles.

Care In Captivity

Mud turtles are a species of semi-aquatic turtles that inhabit a variety of habitats, including wetlands, streams, ponds, and lakes. These tortoises are acclimated to both aquatic and terrestrial environments, and they are active throughout the entire year. Both plant and animal matter are consumed by mud turtles.

Popular as pets, mud turtles require specialized care to guarantee their health and well-being. Mud turtles in captivity require an environment that closely resembles their natural habitat. This includes an aquatic habitat with modest water depth and a terrestrial habitat with abundant concealment places, basking spots, and excavating areas.

The water in the aquatic area should be kept pure, filtered, and between 75 and 80 degrees Fahrenheit. The basking area should be maintained at a temperature of approximately 90 degrees Fahrenheit, and UVB and UVA bulbs should be used for illumination.

Mud turtles ought to be served a variety of foods, such as live insects, nematodes, fish, aquatic vegetation, and commercial turtle pellets. To ensure that the turtle is obtaining a balanced diet, it is necessary to provide a variety of nutrients.

In addition, calcium supplements should be added to their diet to maintain the health of their shells. As they are readily agitated, mud turtles should be handled with caution. Use two hands to support the carapace when handling a mud turtle, and avoid crushing the animal. Furthermore, mud turtles should not be exposed to direct sunlight, as it can cause them to overheat.

Lastly, mud turtles should not be housed with other turtle species. Because they are potentially aggressive and can attack and bite other turtles. It is preferable to maintain mud turtles in their natural habitat, separate from other turtle species.

Housing

The mud turtle is an aquatic turtle species native to the United States, Mexico, and Central America. The carapace of the mud turtle can attain a maximum length of eight inches.

They are omnivorous, consuming small fish, invertebrates, and plants. Typically, mud turtles inhabit modest, transient, and permanent freshwater habitats.

To endure and flourish, mud turtles require a specific form of habitat. In captivity, mud turtles should be provided with a habitat that is at least twice as large as their carapace. A glass aquarium or plastic container with a secure closure that allows the turtle to move freely but prevents escape can be used. The enclosure should contain at least three inches of clean, dechlorinated water, as well as numerous pebbles and concealing places for the turtle to investigate. The enclosure should be kept spotless and the water should be changed frequently to prevent the development of pathogens and vegetation.

The water in the enclosure should be maintained between 70 and 80 degrees

Fahrenheit, while the temperature of the basking area should be between 80 and 90 degrees. Using a submersible radiator, aquarium thermometer, and UVB lighting, the enclosure should be kept at the proper temperature and illumination.

Mud turtles require a high-protein diet and should be served fish, worms, and vegetables in small portions. In addition, the turtle must have access to a calcium supplement to assure appropriate carapace and bone development.

With the proper habitat, sustenance, and temperature, mud turtles can be maintained in captivity for decades. A mud turtle can live for up to 30 years with appropriate care.

Diet

Mud turtles are omnivorous reptiles that consume numerous foods. In slow-moving streams, ponds, and marshes, they subsist on aquatic vegetation, invertebrates, carrion, small vertebrates, and amphibians. Mud turtles are opportunistic consumers, which means they consume whatever is present in their environment.

Mud turtles eat aquatic vegetation like phytoplankton, aquatic insects and larvae, mollusks, snails, worms, crustaceans, tadpoles, amphibians, salamanders, and fish. Additionally, they consume tiny mammals and birds, such as rodents, voles, and songbirds. Mud turtles may also consume the remains of larger animals.

Mud turtles can be served a variety of nutrients in captivity, including small portions of fish, earthworms, crickets, and other invertebrates. Also available are commercial turtle diets, which should be supplemented with fresh fruits and vegetables.

Mud tortoises require a diet that is high in protein, limited in fat, and rich in vitamins and minerals. A poor diet can result in nutritional deficiencies, which can cause health issues such as deformed shells, discoloration, and stunted growth.

For a healthy and content mud turtle, it is essential to provide a balanced and varied diet. Feeding them the proper foods in the proper quantities will help ensure that they remain healthy and active.

Socialization

Mud turtles are tiny aquatic reptiles belonging to the Emydidae family. Their stature may be minuscule, but their social behavior is quite complex. Their socialization involves multiple behaviors that are vital to the survival of the species.

Mud turtles inhabit wetlands and large, shallow waters. Typically, they are reclusive creatures, but during the mating season, they congregate in large clusters. These groups are known as "rafts" and consist of both male and female turtles. Throughout the reproductive season, tortoises engage in intricate social interactions. Males will exhibit behaviors such as head swaying and biting to attract the attention of females and assert their dominance. Females choose partners according to the size, hue, and contour of the male's cranium.

Mud turtles are known to communicate with one another using a variety of vocalizations, including chirps, hisses, and calls. They also employ body language, such as swinging their heads and waving their tails, to display aggressive behavior or seduce a potential mate.

Mud turtles are another species that are known to participate in ritualized forms of battle.

Conflicts like this have a societal purpose in addition to the more obvious one of determining who is dominant. The bouts provide the tortoises the opportunity to assess one another's prowess and create a social order inside the raft by putting their findings to the test.

Mud turtles are known to participate in a wide variety of activities, the most notable of which is their social activity. They feed on water plants and animals, particularly crabs, invertebrates, and tiny fish. In addition, to maintain a healthy internal temperature, they will sunbathe on logs or boulders.

The ecology of wetlands depends heavily on the presence of mud turtles. They do this by grazing on aquatic species that are lower on the food chain, which helps to maintain the balance of the food chain. In addition to this, they protect water wildlife such as fish and amphibians that live in the area.

The social behavior of mud turtles may be described as both complex and fascinating. It is vital to the continuation of the species and elucidates the particular behavior of the aquatic animals in question, both of which are crucial to their existence.

CHAPTER FOUR

Breeding

Mud turtles are an endemic species of freshwater turtle found in North, Central, and South America. They are terrestrial turtles of medium size with a smooth, flattened carapace. The mud turtle is an omnivore, which means it consumes both plant and animal matter. As long as the environment is properly prepared, it is not difficult to breed these tortoises.

Successful reproduction of mud turtles requires a temperature gradient between 70 and 85 degrees Fahrenheit and a humid environment. The temperature of the water should be maintained between 70 and 80 degrees Fahrenheit. In the enclosure, there should be a shallow water area with a depth of two to four inches.

Additionally, the enclosure should be furnished with a slightly elevated basking area. This area should be maintained between 85 and 90 degrees Fahrenheit.

Male and female mud turtles should be placed in the same enclosure to initiate reproduction. The male will approach the female mud turtle and attempt to allure her by swimming around her and swaying his head. If the female is receptive, she will permit the male to mount and copulate with her.

Typically, female mud turtles deposit eggs in the spring or early summer. Typically, the ova are deposited in saturated soil or sand and should be incubated between 82 and 85 degrees Fahrenheit. Typically, incubation lasts 10 to 12 weeks.

Once the hatchlings emerge, they should be housed in a separate enclosure containing abundant vegetation and shallow water. They will need a place to bask and a diet of plant matter and small invertebrates.

In conclusion, it is not difficult to propagate mud turtles if the appropriate environment is provided. Providing a temperature gradient, a shallow water area, and a basking area will aid in the reproduction and hatching of aquatic organisms.

Courtship And Mating

Mud turtles are small, semi-aquatic turtles that inhabit marshes and wetlands, among other slow-moving bodies of water. They favor shallow, vegetated waters and can be observed basking on pebbles and logs near the water's edge. Mud turtles are distinct among turtles in that they do not migrate to reproduce, preferring to remain in the same location throughout the year.

Similar to other turtles, mud turtles reach sexual maturity between 3 and 5 years of age and participate in a courtship ritual. A male turtle will approach a female turtle, circle her, and wave his head and appendages to attract her attention. If the female is receptive, the male will mount her and perform a brief courtship act consisting of striking his front feet on her carapace or cranium.

Typically, the actual coupling of mud turtles occurs in the water. The female will deposit her eggs in a clay or sand burrow that she has excavated herself. The male will then fertilize the embryos, after which the female will cover them with soil. The female will then abandon the nest, allowing the eggs to hatch independently.

The maximum lifespan of a mud turtle is 30 years in captivity and 20 years in the open. Generally, they are reclusive creatures, but during the reproductive season, they can be seen in tiny clusters. In addition to being opportunistic consumers, they will consume anything they can get their paws on, including fruits, vegetables, insects, nematodes, and small fish.

Egg Laying And Incubation

To propagate, mud turtles deposit embryos. Typically, the female lays two to three eggs per brood in late spring or early summer. The eggs are typically deposited in a shallow nest of clay or sand near a source of fresh water. During the summer months, a female may deposit multiple eggs. Depending on the species and environmental temperature, the embryos will incubate for between two and three months.

Once the embryos have been deposited, the mother can no longer assist in their incubation. The ova must rely on their environment for protection and temperature maintenance. The soil or sediment insulates the eggs, while the moisture keeps them hydrated. The environment's temperature will determine how rapidly the embryos incubate. If the temperature is too high, the embryos may develop too rapidly, causing deformities or mortality. If the temperature is too low, it is possible that the embryos will not develop.

Once the eggs have been adequately incubated, the hatchlings will burrow their way out of the nest. The juvenile tortoises will be left alone and will have to fend for themselves. They consume insects, nematodes, and other microscopic animals. They will migrate to larger bodies of water and begin feasting on larger prey as they mature.

Mud turtles are generally easy to care for in captivity. They are resilient organisms that require little upkeep. They require a large aquarium with numerous concealment spots and a substrate such as gravel or sand. They also require a place to bask and a water source. They thrive on a diet that includes nematodes, invertebrates, and commercial turtle delicacies.

The mud turtle is a resilient and adaptable species that can exist in captivity without difficulty. With appropriate maintenance and care, these tortoises can live for decades. They are an excellent option for novices who wish to maintain a companion turtle.

Caring For New Hatchling

Caring for a mud turtle hatchling is a huge responsibility, but it can also be extremely rewarding. Native to North America, mud turtles are a species of semi-aquatic freshwater turtle.

They are resilient, active, and simple to maintain.

When setting up a tank for a mud turtle for the first time, it is essential to choose the correct size and type of aquarium. A 10-gallon aquarium is sufficient for one mud turtle hatchling. The aquarium should be densely populated with aquatic vegetation, along with pebbles, detritus, and other ornaments. The temperature of the water should be between 75 and 85 degrees Fahrenheit, and it should be filtered.

Dietary requirements for mud turtles include aquatic invertebrates, crustaceans, earthworms, and commercial turtle pellets. It is important not to overfeed the turtle, as this can lead to health problems. In addition, regular partial water changes should be performed to keep the water pure.

Because mud turtles are social creatures, it is essential to provide them with a basking spot. Place a basking boulder or pedestal near a heat source to achieve this. The light should be turned on for 10 to 12 hours every day.

In addition to being sensitive to the environment in which they live, mud turtles need their tank to be immaculate. To do this, regular water changes, tank cleanings, and the removal of any uneaten food as well as other debris are required.

Last but not least, mud turtles need to be taken to the veterinarian regularly. This involves getting regular checkups as well as vaccines and testing for parasites. In addition to this, it is necessary to keep a constant eye on the health of the turtle and respond appropriately to any symptoms that may indicate sickness.

A freshly born mud turtle requires a lot of attention and care, which may be a very pleasant experience but also a huge commitment. You can guarantee that your mud turtle has a long and healthy life by providing it with an appropriate habitat and the food it needs.

CHAPTER FIVE

Threats

Small mud turtles inhabit wetlands, ponds, and slow-moving streams. They are omnivores, consuming insects, nematodes, and plants. Although they are not popular as companions, they can be fascinating additions to an aquarium. Unfortunately, in the environment, mud turtles encounter some dangers that can severely reduce their population size.

The destruction and degradation of their natural habitat are one of the greatest hazards to mud turtles. Wetlands and slow-moving streams are frequently dredged or filled in to make way for agriculture and development. This habitat loss can deprive mud turtles of the resources they require to survive.

Pollution is a significant hazard to mud turtles. Oil, pesticides, and fertilizers can contaminate mud turtles' drinking water and sustenance sources. This contamination can make mud turtles sick or even kill them.

There are numerous predators of mud turtles, including raccoons, skunks, and larger turtles. These predators can decimate populations of mud turtles if their populations are not managed.

Mud turtles are frequently harvested for the pet trade and their flesh. This harvesting has the potential to reduce the number of mud turtles in the environment and induce local extinctions.

Climate Change: Climate change can cause droughts and other changes in weather patterns, which can disrupt mud turtles' wetland habitats. This can make it more challenging for mud turtles to locate sustenance and shelter, and can even result in their demise.

If left unchecked, these hazards can have a devastating impact on mud turtle populations. It is essential to take measures to protect and conserve mud turtle habitats and to regulate mud turtle harvesting.

Conservation Efforts

In many areas, mud turtles are considered imperiled or endangered due to habitat devastation, pollution, and human and animal predation. Therefore, conservation efforts have been implemented to aid in the protection of these extraordinary organisms.

Habitat restoration and preservation is one of the most effective conservation measures for mud turtles. This includes the creation and maintenance of wetland areas, the preservation of extant wetlands, and the restoration of degraded wetlands. In addition, mud turtles require access to shallow water, so the creation and maintenance of shallow water areas is essential. This can be accomplished by utilizing artificial ponds, riverbanks, and other modest water areas.

Reducing environmental pollution is an additional essential conservation effort. This can be accomplished by restricting the application of fertilizers, pesticides, and other contaminants. In addition, reducing water discharge and increasing water filtration can help reduce the number of contaminants in water.

Lastly, it is essential to regulate the harvesting of mud turtles in areas where they are prevalent. This can be accomplished by regulating and licensing harvesters of mud turtles.

In addition, there are laws prohibiting the hunting or capture of mud turtles for commercial purposes.

Overall, conservation efforts for mud turtles are necessary to prevent further damage to these animals. By implementing habitat restoration, reducing pollution, and regulating the harvesting of mud turtles, we can help ensure that these incredible creatures will flourish in the environment for many years to come.

Economic Impacts

Mud turtles are a species of freshwater reptile that can be found worldwide. These tortoises serve a vital role in the ecosystem, as they provide sustenance for birds and other animals and are an integral part of the food chain. In addition to their ecological significance, mud turtles can have economic consequences.

Local communities can derive a source of income from mud turtles. Mud turtles are harvested for sustenance and traditional medicine in numerous regions of the globe. They are also frequently sold as pets because they are simple to care for and require little space. This can provide locals who acquire and sell tortoises with a source of income.

Aquaculture can also utilize mud turtles. They can serve as a food source for fish and help control algae and plant growth in reservoirs. This can aid in enhancing the productivity of aquaculture operations, resulting in higher profits for local producers.

Additionally, mud turtles can help control insect infestations. As they prey on small insects, they can aid in the control of parasite populations in areas where they are prevalent.

This can help reduce the need for chemical pesticides, which can be costly and have negative environmental effects.

Lastly, earth turtles can attract visitors to local regions. Since they are fascinating to observe, they can attract more visitors to an area, resulting in increased revenue for local businesses.

Overall, mud turtles can have a positive effect on the local economy. By providing a source of income, controlling vermin, and attracting vacationers, they can contribute to the economic growth of the community.

Common Health Problems

Mud turtles are small aquatic turtles found throughout the United States in ponds, lakes, rivers, and marshes. These turtles are exceptionally adaptable and can persist in a wide range of aquatic habitats. Sadly, they are also susceptible to a variety of health issues.

Poor water quality, inadequate nutrition, and absence of exercise are the leading causes of health problems in mud turtles. Poor water quality can result in bacterial and fungal infections, which can cause respiratory issues, skin irritation, and deformities in shells. Inadequate nutrition can result in insufficient carapace growth, a lack of appetite, and poor body condition. Lastly, a lack of physical activity can result in muscle atrophy, poor carapace shape, and stunted growth.

In addition to these prevalent problems, mud turtles are susceptible to parasites such as tapeworms, roundworms, and flukes. These parasites can result in anemia, lethargy, weight loss, skin irritation, and deformed shells.

It is essential to closely monitor the health of your mud turtle and to provide appropriate nutrition and a healthy environment. Regular visits to the veterinarian can aid in diagnosing and treating health problems before they become severe. In addition, you must provide your tortoise with clean water, a nutritious diet, and sufficient space for exercise. By providing proper care, you can ensure that your mud turtle stays healthy and content.

Conclusion

The mud turtle is an essential member of the reptile family, playing a crucial function in its ecosystem. It is a distinctive animal due to its ability to survive in and around water, and its diminutive size makes it simple to observe. Its diet consists of a diversity of aquatic invertebrates, snails, and worms, contributing to the ecosystem's equilibrium.

Its primary predators are raccoons, skunks, and foxes, which contribute to population control. Even though mud turtles are relatively common, habitat loss and pollution threaten their ability to survive. There is a need for conservation efforts to assure their long-term survival.

Overall, the mud turtle is an intriguing creature that contributes significantly to the ecosystem. It is a wonderful animal to observe and appreciate, and its preservation is vital to maintaining its population. With appropriate protection and management, the mud turtle can flourish in its natural habitat for many years to come.

Understanding The Unique Needs

Since mud turtles are semiaquatic, they require both land and water habitats to survive. It is essential to provide them with the proper environment to ensure their happiness and well-being. To provide them with the best possible care, it is also essential to comprehend their specific requirements.

The habitat of mud turtles must contain both land and water. They require a modest body of tepid water, such as a pond or aquarium, in which to swim and hunt for sustenance. They should be able to navigate on the bottom of the water, as they spend considerable time out of the water. Additionally, the water should be regularly filtered and replaced.

Land habitats for mud turtles should provide ample concealment and basking locations. This can be accomplished by decorating the tank with pebbles, logs, and other objects. It is essential to provide sufficient concealing places so that the turtle feels safe and secure. Additionally, mud turtles require a basking platform to rinse off and warm up.

The basking platform should be elevated above the water's surface and offer the turtle a comfortable, dry place to rest.

The majority of a mud turtle's diet must consist of animal proteins, such as nematodes, crickets, and other tiny invertebrates. Additionally, they will consume plant matter, such as lettuce and other vegetables. It is essential to provide a variety of foods to ensure that their nutritional requirements are met.

Due to the sensitivity of mud turtles to tension, it is essential to provide them with a tranquil environment. Extremely distressing for them are loud sounds and abrupt movements, so it is best to avoid them whenever possible. It is also essential to provide them with a secluded sleeping area, such as a dark corner of the aquarium or a cave-like structure.

As they are social animals, mud turtles should be kept in groups of at least three or four. As congestion can lead to tension and conflict, it is essential to provide sufficient space for each turtle to have its area.

In conclusion, mud turtles require a habitat with both land and water, a diversity of nutrients, an abundance of concealment places and basking areas, and a serene and calm atmosphere. It is also essential to provide them with sufficient space to move around and enough companions to ensure their happiness and health. With proper care, mud turtles can be excellent companions.

Adopting

Mud turtles are an ideal companion for those in search of a novel and rewarding experience. In addition to being intriguing to observe, they can also be quite entertaining. Despite being comparatively small and innocuous, mud turtles are notoriously difficult to handle due to their inherent aggression.

Adopting a mud turtle is a wonderful way to bring vitality into your household. In general, mud turtles are simple to care for, but ensuring their health and safety does require some knowledge and effort. Here are a few considerations when adopting a mud turtle:

Provide a large habitat for your mud turtle – Mud turtles require ample space to move around, so it is essential to provide them with a habitat that is large enough to meet their requirements. A large aquarium or terrarium is ideal, as it will give your companion ample space to move around and provide you with an excellent view of it.

Provide a shallow pool of water – Mud turtles must be able to submerge in water, so provide them with a shallow pool of water to swim in. The optimal pool depth is at least four inches.

Provide the appropriate diet – Mud turtles require a high-protein, calcium-rich diet. A healthy diet should include worms, crickets, and other invertebrates in addition to dark verdant vegetables. Avoid feeding them fish, as doing so can cause a variety of health issues.

Monitor their temperature and humidity - To flourish, mud turtles require specific temperatures and humidity levels. Ensure that the temperature of their habitat remains between 73 and 85 degrees Fahrenheit. The relative humidity should range between 60 and 80 percent.

Provide a basking area – To remain healthy, mud turtles must be able to luxuriate in the sun. Provide a comfortable and dry location for your turtle to bask. This will contribute to their health and happiness.

By adhering to these guidelines, you can provide your mud turtle with a secure and comfortable habitat. Adopting a mud turtle can be a rewarding and delightful experience; however, you must ensure their health and safety before doing so.

THE END

Printed in Great Britain
by Amazon

24375263R00036